TO BUSTER, INKY & GINGER

# Will Moses
# RAINING CATS & DOGS

SCHOLASTIC INC.
New York  Toronto  London  Auckland
Sydney  Mexico City  New Delhi  Hong Kong

## GONE TO THE DOGS

Means: A place has deteriorated or
fallen apart.

Neighbors gossiped that ever since the
Joneses moved away, their house had
gone to the dogs.

## IN A PICKLE

Means: Someone's in big trouble!

Friends warned Maybelle: "Don't balance on the
rim of that barrel, Maybelle!" Now she's really in
a pickle.

## RAINING CATS AND DOGS

Means: Raining heavily.

The Beverly sisters insisted on walking to church even though it was raining cats and dogs.

## FEELING BLUE

Means: Feeling sad.

Just thinking about six more weeks of winter had poor old Ben and his cat and dog—and mouse—feeling blue.

## HIGH AND DRY

Means: Being left without a means to survive.

"No food, no map, and now no water! Methinks we've been left high and dry!" the captain said.

## SHIPSHAPE

Means: Being neat, tidy—and ready to go.

Captain Smucker smiled to see his shipshape ship all scrubbed, trimmed and ready to sail.

## MAKE A BEELINE

Means: Head straight for something—as quick as you can!

Buzz was tired of the city and intended to make a beeline for the country.

## BRING HOME THE BACON

Means: Bring home the paycheck for hard work done.

Yes, ma'am, you could always count on hardworking Bob to bring home the bacon.

## GET THE BALL ROLLING

Means: To get things started.

When it came to winter games, those country boys sure knew how to get the ball rolling.

## GET YOUR GOAT

Means: To push a game far enough to get someone mad.

When that ogre came by, stealing whatever he saw, he really got Farmer Brown's goat!

## HORSING AROUND

Means: Just playing around.

Everyone thought Great-Aunt Zelda was just horsing around when she entered the Derby, but she won!

## RED HERRING

Means: A clue that has nothing
to do with the mystery
or situation at hand.

A rgh . . . ," the mate said.
"Maybe those fish are
just red herrings; maybe there's
something else we should be
worrying about."

## HOOK, LINE AND SINKER

Means: Believing someone's tall tale—
wholeheartedly.

Those gullible fish fell for the fisherman's trick, hook, line and sinker!

## HANGING BY A THREAD

Means: Leaving someone in suspense.

Timothy Mouse wasn't sure if he was going to escape Tom Cat or not; he was left hanging by a thread.

## GOING IN THE HOLE

Means: Spending more money than you have! Oops!

The miners went in the hole to buy that mine—luckily they struck gold!

## SPILL THE BEANS

Means: Someone is supposed to keep a secret—but instead tells all.

What was in the pail was supposed to be a secret, until Georgiana spilled the beans and told *everybody.*

## SHORT FUSE

Means: Someone easily loses his temper— zip!

The Badden brothers were a match for the principal. What they didn't know was—he had a short fuse.

## OUT OF THE WOODS

**Means:** A person has a big problem and finally solves it.

Hansel and Gretel defeated the wicked witch, but they knew they were really out of the woods when they saw the lights of their own cottage.

## CAN OF WORMS

Means: A decision that just creates more problems.

Inviting troublemakers Jake and John to the fancy party was like opening a can of worms.

## SOUR GRAPES

Means: Resenting that someone else wins or takes a prize—and acting like you didn't want it anyway.

It was just sour grapes that made Little May say, "I didn't want that ugly ribbon anyway!" when her totally original grape jam didn't win a prize at the 4-H fair.

SOUR GRAPE JELLY

MADE WITH PURE SOUR GRAPES WITH 100% NATURAL Spite, Anger & Irrational behavior

JUST THE THING TO START YOUR BAD DAY!

FOR PEOPLE WHO FACE DAILY DISAPPOINTMENT

## BUTTERFLIES IN THE STOMACH

Means: Someone is very very nervous about something.

Big Ralph was always so nervous about going to see Dr. Trueblood that he got butterflies in his stomach.

## SEAL OF APPROVAL

Means: Some kind of note or reward that says to the recipient: Good job!

Sammy performed so well at the aquarium that he got the trainer's seal of approval: ten mackerel and a pat on the head.

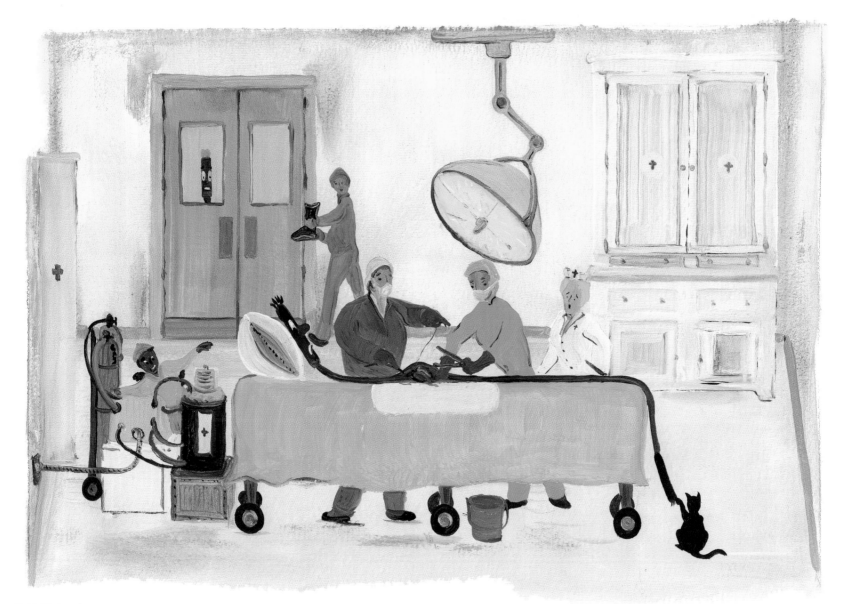

## OPERATING ON A SHOESTRING

Means: Getting something done with very little money.

Ever since the hurricane hit the hospital, the poor doctors had to operate on a shoestring.

## KICK THE BUCKET

Means: A sassy way of saying someone died.

Old Joe Pie and his big black hearse were always ready for someone to kick the bucket.

## BOOKWORM

Means: A person who loves reading so much, he or she always has a book in their hands.

Hector Vector was a real bookworm; he always had his nose in a book.

## THE LAST STRAW

Means: A person's patience has finally run out.

Having his shoelaces tied together was the last straw: How could Tom the Piper's son possibly win?

## TEN-FOOT POLE

Means: How far someone *wouldn't* go to touch something
he or she *doesn't* want to touch.

I wouldn't touch those skunks with
a ten-foot pole!" Harry said
to his brother.

## WHITE ELEPHANT

Means: An object that sticks out and has no use at all.

No circus wanted Jumbo even if he could twirl rings on his trunk; he was just one more white elephant.

## WOLF AT THE DOOR

Means: Hard times are upon a person or family.

The three little pigs had run out of logs for their fire, food for their cupboard and oil for their lamps; they just knew the wolf was at the door.

## LOOK ALIVE

Means: Perk up!

"Look alive!" Dr. Frankenstein said to his monster, as he threw the electrical switch.

## A BARREL OF LAUGHS

Means: Someone is so much fun that everyone laughs.

No question, the Three Stooges are just one big barrel of laughs!

## MY CUP OF TEA

Means: One person is just right for another.

Witch Hazel looked at the toad and said, "Prince, you are *my* cup of tea."

## WARTS AND ALL

Means: A person likes another person for all the good things about him—and all the not-so-good things!

On their wedding day, Tommy Toad married Tina Toad, warts and all.

## BAD EGG

Means: A person is just plain trouble—right from the beginning.

When Louie started squawking no matter how much he was fed, all the other chicks knew he was a bad egg.

## EGG ON YOUR FACE

Means: Being embarrassed—or humiliated—by something you've done or said.

Senator Featherbrain said he did not have a pet chicken, but when the wind blew his hat off and revealed the chicken, he sure had egg on his face.

## A LOAD OFF YOUR SHOULDERS

Means: Something happens to take your worries away.

Plump Jake never thought he'd make it to the top of the mountain, but he did. What a load off his shoulders!

## KNOCK YOUR SPOTS OFF

Means: This will really surprise you.

When it came to boxing, everyone thought Lucky Leopard was champ, but when the match was over, Larry Lion had won! The surprise victory knocked everyone's spots off, including Lucky's.

## IN THE DOGHOUSE

Means: Someone is in big trouble with someone else.

When Papa got home late from bowling, he was in the doghouse with Mama, who had kept supper warm for him.

## GET UP ON THE WRONG SIDE OF THE BED

Means: When a person gets up grumpy and feels as if he or she will be grumpy all day.

It seemed old grumpy Will always got up on the wrong side of the bed, but this time his children were waiting for him.

## SKELETONS IN THE CLOSET

Means: You have a secret that you've kept hidden!

We'd all heard the rumors that Aunt Louise had skeletons in her closet—secrets no one knew. But, by George, this time it was true.

## SOMETHING IS FISHY

Means: Something just doesn't seem right.

Elmer, the night watchman, felt like something was fishy at the aquarium; he never suspected a cat burglar.

## MAKE A BIG SPLASH

Means: Get a lot of attention!

Molly Margaret made a big splash in her neighborhood when she got the only pool on the street.

## COLD FEET

Means: When someone brave suddenly loses their nerve.

*Why not go swimming in January,* old Charlie thought, but when he saw the ice on the pond—and the two toothy fish—he got cold feet.

## UP A POLE

Means: The place someone is driven when all his or her patience is gone.

The weather was hot, the kids were rotten, the dog was howling. It all drove Mother right up a pole.

## ON THE BALL

Means: When someone is quick to understand or does *everything* just right.

Spry old Mr. Murdock was still on the ball at one hundred!

## BULL BY THE HORNS

Means: When someone steps up and tries to solve a
problem on the spot.

Tex was my man; whatever problem arose on the ranch,
he just took the bull by the horns and solved it.

BAG OF SECRETS

## LET THE CAT OUT OF THE BAG

Means: Someone sworn to secrecy has let the secret get out.

It's Warden Jones' fault; no one knew what secret was in
the sack until he let the cat out of the bag.

## THE WRITING ON THE WALL

Means: You can see ahead just what and when the ending will be.

She knew it was the end of the book even before it came: She could just see the writing on the wall.

# INDEX

# BIBLIOGRAPHY

Brenner, Gail. *Webster's New World American Idioms Handbook*. Indianapolis: Wiley Publishing, Inc., 2003.

Collis, Harry, and Mario Risso. *101 American English Idioms*. Chicago: McGraw-Hill, 1987.

Flavell, Linda, and Roger Flavell. *Dictionary of Idioms and Their Origins*. London: Kyle Cathie Ltd., 2006.

*Patricia Lee Gauch, Editor*

ISBN 978-0-545-28105-8

12 11 10 9 8 7 6 5 4 3 2 1                    10 11 12 13 14 15/0

Printed in the U.S.A.                    08

This edition first printing, September 2010

Design by Semadar Megged
Text set in Cheltenham Old Style
The art was done in oil on Fabriano paper.

37